YASHARA SHAMS

BLUEROSE PUBLISHERS
India | U.K.

Copyright © Yashara Shams 2023

All rights reserved by author. No part of this publication may be reproduced, stored in a retrieval system or transmitted in any form or by any means, electronic, mechanical, photocopying, recording or otherwise, without the prior permission of the author. Although every precaution has been taken to verify the accuracy of the information contained herein, the publisher assume no responsibility for any errors or omissions. No liability is assumed for damages that may result from the use of information contained within.

BlueRose Publishers takes no responsibility for any damages, losses, or liabilities that may arise from the use or misuse of the information, products, or services provided in this publication.

BLUEROSE PUBLISHERS
www.BlueRoseONE.com
info@bluerosepublishers.com
+91 8882 898 898
+4407342408967

ISBN: 978-93-93386-33-5

Printed in INDIA

Cover design: Tahira
Typesetting: Tanya Raj Upadhyay

First Edition: August 2023

About Me

My name is Yashara Shams. I was born in Allahabad, Uttar Pradesh, India. I started writing in my early childhood days. In grade three a poem named 'Rain' was in my English books where a very specific question challenged me to write a poem of my own. The question asked me to write my own poetic interpretation of rain. And that's how my love for poetry came into shape. Thus, my first poem was titled 'Rain' and I admit with all pride that it was imperfect. I believe that in literature, poetry is supposed to be imperfect, abstract, born out of the wild, born to stand out.

I have loved reading since the beginning. My parents used to get me books with poems and stories and I read them to sleep. It was a routine that I fell in love with. Growing up, the stories I heard and stories I experienced, I collected them, made them into little snippets, and put them into parts of my poetries. Initially, I was shy to show them to my parents and relatives, but gradually with the unwavering support from my family, I got the courage to have people read it and I would say that they liked it. A lot of people, especially my family have been the founding pillars of my love for poetry. This book and I would not be where I am without them.

The lines that are written in clear letters on clean pages have come a long way from being scribbled in the back of my notebooks and the diary I took to school, sitting in playgrounds just walking down an abyss of comfort and solace.

There are no titles in the poems because I do not want to put a limitation on your minds. I have a strong belief that our minds should not have any boundaries as there are no boundaries to the vast universe and it continues to astound us to this day.

There is no limit to poetry, literature, and art. I've tried to apply that to not only the poetries that are written in this book but to anyone who has entered this realm because it is a healthy addiction that will not only lead them to heal, comfort, warm hugs, sunshine, rainbows and all the things that make them happy. I've tried to give my best in this book and I hope that readers will appreciate it.

A person is a bundle of mistakes and I am sure I might have committed errors here and there. In that regard, all your suggestions are highly welcome.

I may be contacted at yasharashams2@gmail.com

1

Just like the freckles on the moon,
You have those little imperfections,
And those imperfections are the ones,
That makes you more perfect than ever.
When you look in the mirror,
Do you see?
Those wrinkles by your eyes
That appears when you smile?
They give me life.
The way your eyes sparkle
When you're excited
Give me all the more reason to strive.
The way you scrunch your nose,
When you pretend to be angry,
Makes me laugh all the more.
And your smile.
That darned smile.
No adjective I'll ever use
Would be able to match its   perfection.
For your smile is incomparable,
Even to the brightest sun.

2
∞

She knows my past better than me
She knows my destiny,
I hope she forever stands by me,
Cause I won't be where I am,
Without her.
Without her I would die internally,
Every second would feel longer than eternity.
Without her, I would fall apart,
Every moment,
Worse than the last.
Every fraction of my breath,
Piercing through my heart.
Her heartbeat is the only thing,
That keeps me going,
Cause just like my sister,
She's the sibling God forgot to give me.
A simple text of her can make me smile throughout the day,
With her I found solace where I thought I never may.
Everyone sees but only she notices,

Every fake smile I wear,
Every tear conceals itself in the folds of eyes just near.
Keep smiling at me love.

3

In my heart,
In this garden of loneliness,
Blooms another withered flower,
And as the petals fall down,
Once again
Thorns are the only things that remain.
And yet again,
Tired and broken,
Tired of breaking over and over again,
I hug myself,
I hold myself close,
Fear of letting go evident,
Scared that if I let go,
My heart, it might just fall apart.

It rains endlessly,
Dark clouds are all I can see.
Thundering sounds echo
In the silence
In the loneliness

Surrounding me,
In the loneliness that engulfed me.

I look up to you,
But you smile coldly and turn away,
The coldness cutting me like knives,
And as they say

Sticks and stones may break my bones,
But your mere coldness kills me.
Your touches leave bruises,
Your words silence mine.
You could have been the bright in my dark,
The light in the darkest corners of my heart.
But you chose a different path.
I'm sorry I'm trapped in my past,
I'm sorry it doesn't feel like I'm gonna last,
Yet stupid isn't it,
How I dare to dream about
The tranquil breeze,
The placid seas.

Brave of me,
To dream dreams as thee.
Me smiling from the heart and

Not putting up expressions for people to see
As an intricate piece of art.
But maybe this bravery is
What'll get me through,
Past the highest mountains,
The deepest oceans,
Past the darkest days,
And coldest nights,
Through to the dreams I'm so afraid to see,
The tranquil breeze,
The placid seas.

I walk into the room,
And the endless chatter of people,
The never ending smiles
Surround me,

But yet as I walk into the room full of people,
A strange feeling of loneliness suffocates me.

Now as I stand within my group of friends,
Laughter echoes in the silence surrounding me.
The walls of loneliness breaks
For the blink of an eye,
And the fraction of a second,
I feel like I'm truly alright.
Maybe I could get better.

But the happiness fades away,
As I get flashbacks of what happened,
How hard I broke down last night.
How the silence deafened me when I was alone,

How it creates a weight on my chest,
And how it drags me down.

It feels like I'm in an endless ocean,
The waves crashing down,
Dragging me under it,
A silent scream escapes my lips,
I'm fine but I need you to save me.

For once I wish I could smile from my heart,
Show people truly how much they meant to me from the start.
For once the little girl in me wishes she did more than just exist.
For once she wishes she could heal and start again.

Her heart is a fragile piece of glass
So shattered that
When someone tries
To hold it in their embrace
It didn't hesitate to slash them itself
Maybe they kept on holding it,
Maybe let go.
But it still hurts like never before.

She didn't want to give up,
She didn't want to break
The promise she made,
The promise of never leaving.

She offered her heart again,
For her heart had boundaries
As high as her affection,
Endless amount of affection and care,
As shards of glass just standing out
Like the tip of an iceberg,

Prevalent yet so disguised.
She never wanted to hurt
Anyone who came close,
She wanted to stay by their side,
She wanted to stay safe
Enveloped in love,
But everyone knew she was merely a puppet,
And that her reins were in her heart…!!!

6

She stood under the sky,
A dark shade of blue.
She thought it was gonna rain,
Didn't know it would cut her through.
It rained shards of glass,
And she struggled to find a place of shade.
A place where she could let herself rest,
Cause she was tired of standing,
Waiting for the soft drops of rain,
The warmth of it's love,
The love in its embrace.

Her shoulders slouched towards the ground,
And she couldn't pick herself up.
For she had the weight of
The glass sky on her shoulders
And whilst the people stood under the sunlight,
Cursing her for being so frail.

She knelt to the ground,
And stood back up again.
Till her knees gave up,
Bruised black and blue,
Just like her soul.

A whisper
"You're gonna be okay" and a smile,
The glass shatters over her
That's the strength in those words
She fails to recognise...!!!

7

She lives with a memory,
So beautiful, yet so painful.
Yeah, sad memories hurt
But happy memories hurt more.

She remembers standing
At the bottom of a rose plant,
A little baby bud blooming at the top,
She didn't care, she was unaware.
Driven, wild, motivated,
She climbed the tough yet delicate shrub.

Each thorn stood guard of something ethereal.
She slipped from the first,
Yet she started again.
The second scraped her limbs,
Yet she started again.

As she got higher,
Her body felt deprived of everything.

Her head spun around,
Her legs ached for, yearning   for solid ground.

She thought she could only find happiness
Only if she could pluck the flower
Claim it, name it as hers

But when she reached the floweret,
Her hands froze
And her heart stopped
When she saw
A nymphalid.
Taking nectar from the blossom

A pang of guilt crossed her soul
Yet a smile adorned her lips
For she had experienced true happiness
In its best eclipse.

8

A history,
Known to no one else,
No one except her.
A memory,
Which beckons her with a loving dream.
A time that passed by,
Leaving her reminiscent of the tears and the smiles.

She'd never thought about it before,
Never had it occurred to her,
That thinking about her past,
May comfort her in ways unimaginable to any soul.

How she made it till now,
How she knows
That she's standing on solid ground.
The people whom she had by her side,
All those looking her in her eyes.

She looks at them,
And she gets the strength to go on,
Because they taught her to never give up,
To never stop going on,
Because they taught her not to drown.
Yes it was her past,
Yes it didn't last.
But somehow she wants
To keep it by her side,
Make it a part of herself,
As she goes on with her life.

I'm an angel,
I'm the devil.
The one who protects you
While you sleep,
The one who haunts you
In your worst dreams.

Oh look at her
How clueless,
How naïve.
It makes me wanna laugh,
How she thinks she can have,
What she thinks she can do   .

Look into the mirror
Into your future
You have two options
A bitter sweetness,
A sweet bitterness.

You're afraid of me
Yet you also trust me?
What kind of
Strange relationship do we have
Come to me,
I will be the worst pain
You'll have ever felt.
But you should still hold onto me
Cause I'm the only one who can,
Make you feel.

10

Have you ever gone stargazing?
When you hang around them,
For tad a bit longer,
Have you ever heard them whispering?
As they form constellations of
Thousands of fairy lights hanging in the sky,
Hanging protectively over you,
Like a warm blanket.
Even though you don't say anything,
They know everything.

And the sheets on the bed are too small
To hold the vast universe inside the heart.
The suns farthest from are here to hear,
The constant conflicts between mind and the soul.

They whisper…
"We are bound to protect you",
As you are another fallen star,
That shone the brightest before its fall.

11

She's much more than a pretty face
When she revels
she sheds her shimmery facade
and conflagrates
Into an embellished illumination,
Into fireworks

12

Reach out and take my hand,
Even though you might be lost in this maze,
The maze which you call your heart,
Why would thou hide in the shadows,
When thy belong in the brightest of stars.

Let me save you,
And be the bright in your dark,
Your lantern that illuminates your heart,
The fire that ignites your soul,
That fire which sets you apart.
That fire that urges you to break through,
The boundaries your inner voice built for you,
The voice that said you're weak,
And would never make it through.

Hold my hand and allow me to walk you through
The toughest maze life holds for you,
And I promise
When you and I make it past,
Past the highest mountains and deepest valleys,

I promise,
The happiness you will get is meant to last.
I promise,
That you would taste the happiness
Of the most intensely dazzling stars.

As you lay back on the grass,
And remember how we started,
And how it was you,
Who was so strong,
And that it was you,
Who made it.

Last night I had a nightmare,
As I stood at the edge of a lair,
There was not much light present,
For my past existed there.

Till now I thought this was a nightmare,
Nobody ever told me,
That maybe if I can't wake up from it,
This nightmare is the painfully cruel reality,
I live in.

14

As long as I'll live,
I'll live for you,
As long as I'll love,
I'll love only you.
Distance can never keep us apart,
For you and I are in each other's hearts,
As long as I'll live,
I'll live for you.

All the good times we have,
Sneaking out in the middle of the night,
Just to sit on a tree branch,
And watch the sun rise.
You are the one person,
Who resides in my heart and mind.

I'm intoxicated by your mere presence,
When you and I are together,
No other being is in existence.
When you and I are together,

It seems like I'm holding the world in my hands,
Because my hand is holding yours,
A confession I wanna make,
No more of my heart is left for you to take,
I'm utterly and irrevocably in love with you.

Sprawled out on the grass,
Hold me in your arms,
Three words echo in my mind,
When you look into my eyes,
"And then always and forever"

15
∞

Tis the nighttime,
Softly the bells chime,
The soft breeze ruffles my hair,
As I hum my favourite tune,
It almost feels like the air is singing along,
Whispering it's notes,
Singing its song.

The moon shines brighter than usual this beautiful night,
And I vividly feel like a senophile,
It's almost like everything's alright.
The trees and the leaves,
The feathers in the wind,
The water rippling in the stream,
Into their trap have allured me,
A trap of euphoria,
A trap of serenity.

The air surrounding me feels heavy,
A strange sense of calmness seeps into me,

Washing away all my worries,
And in that moment,
It's just me.
Me and the leaves,
Me and the trees,
Me and the feathers,
Me and the streams.

A nightingale comes
And settles into the branch towering me,
It's black eyes shining brightly,
As it sings a cadence of melodies,
Just treading on the strings slightly.

It feels like this song is etched into me,
Branded into my memories,
This place has become my abditory,
I've often felt scared of commitment,
Yet I can't help
But fall head over heels for this place,
It's tranquillity.
It's serendipity.

16
∞

She sits in the same playground as she used to,
When she was only two,
Those were the days,
When she could look up and say,
"Mom look at the bird
Soaring so high in the sky-
I'm gonna be there one day"

Time passed by,
People came and went,
But she lost herself,
In a place unknown to her innocent little self,
It hurts when you lose someone,
But when you lose yourself,
It only feels numb.

She stands in the same playground again,
In Front   of the girl from her past she knew,
Unchanged, exactly how she had been.
She wishes she could turn back time,

And comfort her little self,
Cause the morning will come again,
The dreary winter that may reside around you now,
Will also come to an end.

17

Your eyes are so deep,
I could drown just by looking into them.
The little sparkles in your eyes,
Represent the brightest stars in the galaxy
You are an infatuation I have,
Impossible to resist,
Impossible to let go.

As cliché as it may sound,
I wish I could stop time when you are around
And complain about how infectious your smile is,
Making me blush scarlet on the bluest of my days.

When you and I lay back in the warm,
Under the soft evening sky,
Watching the sun go down,
I know there is nothing more I would ask for.

18

Do you remember me
All the time we spent together
All the memories we made together
Did you forget it all
All the laughs we shared,
All the tears that lay lost somewhere,
All the little smiles we passed,
All these memories now create a void in my heart,
I feel incomplete without you,
When you and I are together ,
I feel like we could conquer the world
With no hindrance whatsoever
You may say you don't need me
But I know you and your little white lies better.

I'm losing myself thinking about you,
Wondering to make you stay what it is I should do?
Cause I'm way too selfish to let you go
And I'm way too scared to let you know,
That I need you by my side

That's why I need you to promise me tonight,
Promise me you will forever stay by my side,
Cause everyone else has left,
And me, I still hope everyday, every night.
I hope that you beg to differ,
I hope that you choose to stay.

19

My head spins around in empty circles,
Does it mean I'm living like a robot
If I'm barely living, barely existing.

The water seeps deep into my lungs
When my limp body hits the water,
I scream but no sound resonates,
What would happen they day I lose,
The day I lose my will to fight.
The day my heart gives up.

Shattered and lost,
I'm too tired to go on
Could you save me
Before I completely lose myself,
In a sea of unexplainable blueness.

20

Your angelic eyes
Tear laden leave me parched
Parched for all the words that wouldn't roll off my tongue

The komorebi that your presence brings about
I wouldn't even lie
Scintillates like the water rippling through the stream at the peak of midnight
With the moon on its full course

21

How secretive could you have been?
Pretending like you don't care,
But secretly leaving your scarf when I was cold.
For sending me a cup of coffee,
When I was sick,
For sending little glances my way,
When you knew I was not okay.
You made it look like you left my side
Like your arms would never hold mine
That you would never allow me to lean upon you
But in reality
You left my side to hold me from another
Your arms never held me again
Because your heart was holding me the entire time.
You would never allow me to lean upon you
Because you would keep me strong enough
To never feel the need to do so.
And keep my head high.

You pretended to have a heart of ice
When in reality your disposition was warm
Just like that hug after I saw you
And I said," I missed you like crazy"
"I missed you so much I went crazy"
"I love you so much it drives me crazy."

22

You're like the warm sun
On a cold windy day
You feel like the flower petals
That touch our face
When we walked in the park
You are the warmth
That spreads in our body
When we drink tea on a cold day
You are the smile we see
And it feels like the world would be happier
That the sun would be warmer
That the petals are leaving soft kisses
Whispering everything's okay.

23

Being in love and being high aren't far apart,
You feel euphoric, unstoppable
Out of control, when you fall in love
It's more adrenaline than the roller coaster
The highs, the lows, the twists, the turns
Even the slight bumps.
You're on the ninth cloud
Nothing can ever get you down.

But the person you love snaps you back to reality
It breaks you, you find yourself in a mess
Shattered into a million pieces.

24

There was this one tree
People used to walk by
It looked lifeless, empty
Cause it was naked and bare
People always talked
About taking it to the ground
Where it might actually belong.

But there was a lady
Who went there everyday without fail
And sat beside it for an hour or two
Passer by said she was a little cracked in the head
Sitting by the tree as useless as it had been
For the past four years.

And one enchantingly magical day
The tree was filled with blooms
Of red and yellow and pink and lavender
You couldn't see an empty part of it
Even in the crevices where

The tree never saw any light, felt no warmth,
Were ablaze with the beauty of the flowers   .

Those flowerets were sight never seen before
People now flocked around from all over
Just to have a single view
Of the miraculous affair that took place.

You are just like the tree, you hold within yourself
The brightest blooms of the century
Even if no one believes in you
You believe in yourself.
Cause at the end of the day,
Sometimes the only person you have around you
is you.

25

From the moment I met you
I knew you were too good for me.
You never committed any sin in your past life
That you should deserve to put up with me.

But when we became friends
I finally found the reason of my existence
I actually felt blissful
For it seemed someone loved me
For me.

Our endless talks
And hearty laughs
Make my life unreal.
Because I am so ecstatic
To have come to know
A friend like you actually existed.
Even till today
I question my life
What could I have done
To find your angelic self
In the mess I call my life.

26
∞

People often ask me
Why can't I   be happy?
It's maybe because
When no one was around
It were the demons in my mind
That calmed me down.
They brought me close enough
To trust them
And believe everything they said
I began to find comfort in darkness

And now when I sense a tiny ray of hope,
I retreat into the comfort of the dark
Covered in covers by the demons of my past
The demons that I now call my home.

I'm scared that if I feel joy,
I'll forget the bad times
And you and I know
Such memories don't leave your soul.

And these memories would be the reason
  I'll go back tumbling into the darkness
I was delusional enough to call my home.

27

She's come to you after a long time
She's tired and exhausted
Of the battle she's been fighting all her life
Since the day she learned about herself,
She's been fighting herself too
Daily.

She's shivering
She needs the solace of your words
One whisper
That's all she needs
Tell her she fought hard
And now she can rest her heart.
Cause her head pounds
And her a familiar ache occupies her bones
Her contused body yearns for a rest
Let her know
That it's okay to feel tired
Like there's not an ounce of strength left
That it's okay to be pathetic
And ask for your simple reassurances.

Cause she only has you
And nowhere to go to.
Without you a heart beats alone
In the deserted streets
Scavenging and pining for some warmth
Wishing something would make it come back to life.

28

Each and every time you feel down
Look up at the sky
At night, at dawn
Look at how the stars paint your name
In the boldest letters at the break of dawn
And how the stars illuminate the sky
Just to see a small smile
Light up your face.
Cause even though people in your life
May come and go
The skies hold promises and reassurances
That you're never alone.

They will be your lantern in the darkness
Your comfort when you need it the most
No matter where you are
They will always watch over you from afar
Because seeing a person as beautiful as you in pain
Is a torture they aren't willing to go through.

29

The going is hard
It'll perhaps drag you down
But inspire yourself to work harder
Put in a little extra effort
Climb those two stairs you otherwise would never.

There's so much more to life
than what meets the eye
and even if you may feel down
the weight of the world
sitting on your head making your shoulders droop down
believe me when I say,
The   weight is nothing less than a crown.

30

It's a mess
Her thoughts have engulfed her
Her thoughts have captured her
In a maze
And no matter how fast she runs
They always catch up to   her
Her demons.
"You were never good enough
You never will be
Look at yourself
How ugly you have come to be"
Are the words it whispers to her.

Some days she thinks she's getting better
But in the end
It all comes back to her
All the voices she wishes she could escape from.
Are the voices that that create tsunamis and tornadoes
In the infinite galaxy of thoughts in her head
Those thoughts that fuel the nightmares
She wishes she could wake up from it.

31

Fall in love with yourself
You are perfect my love
With all those little imperfections
You are you
And you are flawless.
And the people?
They won't be there for you when you're in need
But you
You're gonna be there for yourself
In the highs and the lows
Through light and dark
So fall in love with yourself
Love every nook and corner
Unconditionally, irrevocably
Of the body that has brought you to where you are
You deserve this love.

You ask me what I feel
Your mere words make my heart
Fragmented
Join together like puzzle pieces
Before blowing off to the song of the wind.

33

Your dark aura surrounds me
I succumb to you
To your way with me
Cause you are a work of art
And maybe you have a dark heart
But the way your eyes pierce into my soul
Makes me question my existence as a whole.

Aren't those the words you say to me
Each and every day ?
Make me your muse tonight
Let me be yours till daylight
Cause I've never seen myself the way you do
I've never given in to anyone
As I have to you.

It's scary I trust you
But that doesn't change my mind anymore
Than you do
Cause I'm the designer of my own catastrophe

And you?
The heeder of my destiny.

Make me your muse tonight
Let me be yours till daylight
Cause I've never seen myself the way you do
I've never given in to anyone
As I have to you.
I'm yours.

34

My heart's out on my sleeve
Gasping for a single breath
Like an ocean run dry
Empty promises resound
In the void
That fills my heart up to the brim.

Your voice,
Once a lullaby to me
Has taken all my sleep away
For when I hear it
It so happens that life
Is better than dreamland.

35

Love hurts.
So, I let it hurt
How long have you been here for?
How much longer will you stay?
I wanna know.

The blackness prevails like a delicacy
Silk over glass
A mere step induces daggers
Sticking out of the glass
Wrapped in lavender
Tainted with the fingerprints of a lover
Simply complicated as it sounds
It hurts a lot when you are around
But it's the kind of ache
That dulls when I see the stars sparkle in your eyes
And I wonder
How could pain be so perfect
So beautiful, so unreal.

36

Even the stars are silent today
Did they ever speak something you must say
When it came to a heart as beautiful as yours
Even the wind spoke volumes as it flew past.

How did she hope for something so unreal
How did she hope that the planets would align
How did she hope the stars would fall
To make her wish come true
When she was a star herself
And she could fall to make his dreams come true.
Tears make their way
Smooth as pearls
Creating a hole in her chest that refuses to fill up
Yet a small smile finds itself upon her lips
Because his smile said
That he was the happiest that had ever been.

37

I'd say the celestial bodies look beautiful
But they all stare at you tonight
And as I lie down by your side
Your breath mingling with mine
Indeed the moon and stars would die
Just to look at you for one night
A soft melody resonating in the air
Beckoning you into a deep slumber
Into a pit of sweet dreams they call their lair
Let those synchronous notes take
The reins of your heart
And let the sleep cloud over your frantic heartbeats
The ones resounding in my ear
Let it lull your tension away.
A smile illuminates the bow arch of your lips
As two dimples pop in to say goodnight
Keep that smile forever
Don't stop smiling at me.
Goodnight mi Consuela.

<u>*Note:*</u> *mi Consuela – my comfort; my consolation; my comfortable place*

38

He wanted her heart to remain young forever
Maybe freeze it
For a lifetime of forever
Keep her heart to himself
Maybe it was too pure
For the tainted world to lay their hands Upon it
Maybe he knew something she didn't.

Little does he know
Her heart was already his
Buried in snow
Melting only for him.

39

She's so afraid
To fall for someone again
Cause the only way she fell
Was like a shooting star.
That only fell to make someone's wishes come true
Her thoughts call out to him
Like a muted whisper
Blowing away like a feather
She wishes him goodnight
Hopes he sleeps tight
Because he saw a shooting star in
His dream that night.

40

It's been so long
So many things I did wrong
Her seraphic nature making me question my existence
I'd take all types of pain
To turn back time
And make everything all right.

41

She was different
She was unique
She had a fire deep set in her eyes
Not one that could be put out with water
But one
That brought water to ignite.

When the world tried to cut off her voice
And strangle her
It didn't cease the fire
Only fuelled it to grow more.

42

I want to let go
I wanna believe
That I'm finally okay
But my scars are fresh as ever
Expressions are dangerous
For you believe my smile
But my heart doesn't.
Tears and emotions?
Those are history
Not because I don't hurt now
But because I've become used to them.
You can't break me anymore
If someone tries?
They'll fail.
How do you break something
That has already been shattered to pieces?
That's already blown away
To the sound of the gentle wind.

43

Voices that screamed in my head
Stole my happiness
Just because it couldn't find its   own.

Slashed my heart
Till it bled
Till its tears ran dry
Pushed it up to the point
To which it couldn't survive.
Empty heart beats that once resonated in my chest
The silence screeches louder than it ever could.

She sits in her room
The fire in her eyes
It would destroy you before you uttered a word
Wrapped in satin
Neck loaded with diamonds and pearls
She chooses to not beg for mercy from the pain
And she chooses to not be good
For as they said
Well behaved women never made history
And the pain she lives in
She looks at it and smiles
The pain is now her home.
And happiness is intruding.

45

My war with you starts with this breath
The old me is still in me
But she wont come forward when you call
The old caring me
That resided for thee
Is long gone.
The heart that used to shiver within me
It drowned.
And although its' lifeless tears
Still glisten in shades of red
It only makes her sparkle more.

46

I wish I could remember me
Who I was
Before what I came to be.
Like a shrivelled leaf floating in the chilly winter wind
I found myself in a place
Unknown to my own being.

I brought myself to be stepped on
Just to see a spark of delight
Dance across your cheeks
Your smile became my ultimate aim
I'm lost at bay
And the waves rise higher today
And I'm scared just like that
I couldn't see.

I look in your eyes
Hoping to find happiness
But all that looked back at me

47

This is you
You should say it aloud that "this is me"
Not sometimes who you pretend to be.
For you are the definition of art
Even when you're falling apart.
Even when your heart's scattered
In a million pieces
Know that each one has its own tale to tell
Of how you fight the dark everyday
The tale of your legendary war
that ravages your soul.

48

I run along a familiar path,
The air is cold, the ground is wet, the sky is dark,
And the raindrops drizzle on my head.
My legs burn from working so hard,
My heart hurts from breaking apart,
My legs bruised and scraped,
Have no energy to run this race,
Yet I run because this race is like the devil's snare,
And I refuse to lose to my worst nightmare.
My surroundings suddenly change,
I'm no longer standing on a road,
But now I'm on a cliff,
I move two steps forward
Just to meet a vast ocean bed,
The sky is a dark shade of blue,
Almost as blue as the waves crashing below.

The air is still cold,
The ground is still wet,
And all I want to do is forget,

Forget that my past exists,
Forget that I exist.

I inhale sharply,
And hold my breath,
Just to let go
And clear my head
As I jump off the cliff,
The cold air hits my face,
The adrenaline rush comes as expected,
And in that moment I forget,
In that moment I cease to exist.

The water hits my body,
And it drags me down,
It almost feels like an eternity,
As I fight my urge to drown.

My surroundings suddenly change again,
I'm not greeted by cold air or a post rain ground,
But the clear air,
And the soft sunshine of the sun,
Daffodils and tulips smiling brightly,
And me amidst them, holding on barely.

It feels like the sunshine is reaching my soul,
Past the boundaries I've built
To protect my heart
From the daggers of my past.
Healing it, filling it with love,
There's this one rose in the middle of the meadow
Where I stand,
Its different cause it's withered,
One by one its petals fall down,
And a new bud begins to blossom,
I only have one wish
Seeing the rose grow,
May the petals teach me an art,
The art of letting go.

49

You're the light
You're the shine
That illuminates my sky
Every night

You ask me why it is you whom I cling to
You ask my why acknowledging others is something I can't do
You ask me even when I have so many others
Why do I still need you

The tiniest measurable unit of time
Gone without you
Knowing that I hurt you
Is like a knife that stays serrated
Through every wound I ever had
And I want to make it up to you

When sometimes
I may try to hold up a disguise
It could never stop you

And I don't want you to
And after all
After everything
I come back to you

Comfort is all I want you to have
Laughter is all I want you to remember
And us as best friends is all I wish for.

50

You are her bitter sweetness
In this world of billions of people
You've acclaimed her heart
Like you're her personal devil

In this overcrowded room
Yours still glisten in the sultry shadows
Your smile still shines brighter
Than the stars in the northern sky.

51

All she wants from life is to smile
See the sunshine, feel its warmth
She's lived in the dark enough
She's cried enough
She doesn't want to live
She wants to feel alive
Once before she dies
She wishes to have a free life
Spread her wings and soar high
And have no worries
About what would happen
If she jumps off

Probably lost count of times
Tried to get out of this head of mine
My thoughts that captured me
In a prison called my mind

Imprisoned am I
Or is it just a trick of my mind
Depends on how we all perceive ourselves to be.

53

A box
My thoughts limited to it
A sky
The hoard of endless possibilities
A black hole
A place to which I honestly wish I could go

My thoughts were limited
And my thinking was too
My thoughts limited my thinking
If you understand what I mean to say to you.

I wanted to see the world
Outside of the box
Think a little differently
Than what everyone else wanted me to
My wings were broken
But I still wanted to spread them
And learn how to fly.

The dolent me fought valiantly
And yet she's trying to figure out if she won or lost
All I know is I wanted to fly
So I did.

54

She's an angel
She's the devil
The one who protects you when you sleep
The one who haunts you in your worst dreams.

You can choose
A sweet bitterness
Or a bitter sweetness
Take your pick

You're afraid of her
Yet you also resist her?
What is this strange relationship you have
She'll be the worst pain you'll ever feel
But you'll still crave her
Cause she'll be the one who'll at least make you feel something.

55

Could anyone be as deranged as she is
Is it possible?
Do such circumstances exist
Are they plausible?

Bloody are her hands
From the innumerable times she killed her desires
For they all say
Destroy that thing
That destroys you

The highs come as fast as the lows
The mania comes right after the blows
Some days it's   her being the meira she is
Other days her reflection disappears owing to the fact that it doesn't recognize herself.

Some days I wonder
If I should stay
And hope you are okay

Cause I remember the day
You told me
No one ever wanted to stay
By your side

And I wanna tell you it's okay to cry
And scream your emotions out till your throat hurts
I want you to know I'll be right by your side
My shoulder is ready   to be the support you require.

I cross my fingers
Hope that you get the happiness you deserve
Make sure I'll be there to hold you through everything that comes your way.

57

She hurts in broad daylight
She hurts at the brink of midnight
When nobody's there to see her tear laden eyes
The pain cascades down her cheeks
Transforming
Transitioning
They bleed out on paper
Leaving marks like the scars
On her hands and on her heart
And she leaves her room at 3 in the morning
Strokes your hair while you're in deep sleep
And covers you in her love
because she promised to take care of you
And exist for you
Always and forever.

58

Someday when you stumble across these words
I wonder if you would reminisce
That she's that girl who listened to cliché pop songs on repeat
That she's the girl who blushed ever so wildly
That she's that girl who over the fact that she ate too much
Argued with you relentlessly.

I wonder if you remember
That she was the girl
Who clung onto you so hard
Terrified that she was gonna fall apart
I wonder if you reminisce the moment
When your hand slipped from hers
And along with losing
She lost herself completely.

59

If you could,
Would you stop life for a bit?
Allow yourself to take a breath
And rest your weary head?

Because it feels like life is just happening,
And everything is out of control,
And you're just existing in a life,
That doesn't belong to you anymore.
Living like a puppet is humbugging,
And having no strings attached,

You're scared of
Getting your heart broken again,
You tell yourself to stop caring,
But you know you'll never be able to.
You tell yourself to let go,
But you know it's something
You'll never do.

60

.I want to be made up of sunlight
And feel the burn of the sun.
I want to dance amongst the stars
And lose myself in the dark.

61

For a moment,
Let's stop pretending that everything's okay.
I want to break down
And not feel like I'm weak

I'm back under the burning gaze of my four walls,
And this facade we've all been putting up,
It's   starting to show.
The ocean that seethed under a desert
It threatens to break loose.
You and I both know we won't be okay,
But I want you to know I'm there for you.
I want you to know I'm ready to break down,
And it's   okay if you are too.

62

We should reminisce the cold streets we walked through,
Not an ounce of clothing that hung over our bones,
It's   a dolent sight to see,
Something that permanently isn't meant to be.
The tattered windows and doors,
The shards of glass that hold stories galore.
And this caligo that we exist in,
Isn't ours to live in.

63

The lake in the forest,
Up to my nose,
I drown in my own blood.
And even the moon shines red,
And he who hunts me down,
Slashes another gash down my bare chest.
Bruised and cut
My warm pillow floats in my own red blueness,
Fades away into the cold,
And the tears freeze on my cheeks.
Before they even drip down my lips that were so pale,
But from where he stands,
They're so red.
Red enough for him to claim them as his.
Now it's calm.
For no screams would leave my lips,
All my lipsticks they're his now.
He who stands there motionless,
Dreamy, but its a bad dream,
An ascian.

A-

I forgot I can't speak

I don't have a mouth anymore.

64

Someone asked me when I would write my next poem,
And I told them next year.
For each one that I wrote this one,
Hid a small glistening tear.
And the promises I made to myself,
That I would take care of you.
Broke only once and twice and a million times,
And the promise that I would write a poem next year,
Isn't mine anymore .

65

This is insanity
And the thoughts you have
Don't smear upon paper.
And somewhere we drown in places
With splinters down our stretched skin.
Undecorated skin
And we dance in the aura of being lost
Briveting through
Drenched in bare blood and sweat,
Even in the virulent cold.
Down the abyss of I don't   know who I am,
And wanting to throw yourself off of the edge of unforgiving vexation,
This edge that found you in a bottomless chasm,
Barefoot
It's chaotic.

66

The ball and the tulle
Overflowing emotions in a hall overflowing with people.
And you who has grasped my hand
Eyes filled with purely wild innocence for a whirl mid air,
Is it just innocent or tainted with the blood of sin?
Hand on the base of my torso,
Twirling around in unkempt happiness,
And glitters and cheers of the bystanders.
Those brown pupils never leaving mine,
And melting softly into mine,
Pulling you into me,
I whisper,
"I know you hide a dagger somewhere within that glee. "

As the piano chords raise an octave I do too,
And my feet leave the cold tile,
A smile that illuminates your face in mischievous viridity,
"Even if I did I wouldn't tell thee"

And the oath of silence fracts,
I play your game with you now.
My bones are mine and will go with me,
Even if its to decorate my own grave,
Yet why art thou capturing me in an ardor,
It's lucelent,
Just like the dagger as it grazes my lips,
Through the agony,
Slicing through the melody,
Before my blood soils the coruscating jewels on silk and tulle,

67

Its real

When the melody of broken surface tension of tear drops

Doesn't play on the piano.

And I can't see the music

Dance to life in front of my closed eyes.

When the reflection in the mirror,

Waits for two words fall from the lips,

For longer than two seconds.

It's real.

68

There's more blood on my skin,
Than beneath it.
And there are more bandages on my arm,
Than nerves in my body.
No laceration should feel left out,
Like the 10 year old me,
Trembling beneath the sheets,
And the sheets were made of roses.
Those roses' stems.

69

The city of New York
20 something
The streets are singing
The notes to my ears
Are off key.

The bar
With the familiar smile
Hugs
As warm as you'd left them be
But the bitter liquid going down your throat
Isn't bitter anymore.

70

It rained but they couldn't write about the drops against their skin
Or the wistful melodies in the thunder of the rain
Or the yen to feel the grass under their feet
Abashed cheeks under the burning sun
Soft thorns of an abysmal ground,
Never bereft of blandishment,
The air that dug deep into the skin on their faces,
Like an invitation for the blue moonlight,
That claimed them faster than the rabbit claimed the moon.

71

It's beautiful how some people feel like rain
Powerful like the thundering clouds
And coruscating like the flashing bolts
And even though you were crying
And they sweep all your tears away like they were mere drops of the rain
Quenching a dried up lake somewhere
Leaving you smiling
In the middle of nowhere